CAMBRIAN COUNTRY

Welsh Emblems

Cambrian Country
Welsh Emblems

David Greenslade

Published with the aid of
the Arts Council of Wales.

ISBN: 0-86381-613-4

Cover design: Sian Parri

First published in 2000 by
Gwasg Carreg Gwalch, 12 Iard yr Orsaf, Llanrwst, Wales LL26 0EH
01492 642031 01492 641502
books@carreg-gwalch.co.uk Internet: www.carreg-gwalch.co.uk

Some of these paragraphs have appeared in the following places:
Radio Wales, Poetry Wales, Ninnau (USA), H²O (Norway),
Product (Scotland), Waterlog (England).

Contents

Introduction

This is a book about emblems or icons, in the contemporary sense of a voguish term. The word used to have a mostly religious meaning, and when we talked of icons we usually thought of dim, smoke-browned Madonnas in gilded frames, swirled about by incense and ancient music on the iconostases, the icon screens, of candle-lit eastern churches. Nowadays it has much wider connotations. It has entered computer-speak of course, but it also edges away into worlds of allegory, imagery and emblemisation. Cambrian Country is about the allegories, the images and the emblems that constitute an iconography of Wales.

Every people has its icons, and when a people becomes a nation-state its icons are generally sure, decisive and well defined. The national flag is one, of course, the national game another. The national anthem can be an aural icon, the national cuisine an icon of taste. Language, literature, architecture, landscape – all can be elevated into patriotic symbolism, helping to unite a people in pride, loyalty or obedience. From the Eiffel Tower to the World Series, from Sphinx to smorgasbord, from Waltzing Matilda to Red Square to Nelson Mandela to William Shakespeare, the universally known symbols of national identity are ceaselessly cherished and exploited.

They call it 'imaging' in the advertising business, and, God knows ,its effects are not always benevolent. What the icon has lost in spiritual influence it long ago gained in political power. The flag of the United States has acquired such pseudo-sanctity that it is actually illegal to allow it to touch the ground, just as my mother thought it a sin to place a secular book on top of the Holy Bible.

Such is the prime force of the icon in dogmatic or unscrupulous hands: the ambiguous force of patriotism, which can be noble indeed, but can also be perverted into cruel complacency. Crusaders, Communists, imperialists of every kind have harnessed icons as instruments of their ideology. The ideal of the Victorian Royal Navy shared a genre with the heroic proletariat of Stalin's workers' paradise. The cross of St George on Richard the Lionheart's shield had much the same intent as the teeth on a fighter plane in World War II – to make its protagonists feel tremendous, that is, to make its enemies feel small.

Artistically, it may be lucky that Wales is not a nation-state. The icons of power can be very monotonous, sharing as they do an aesthetic of unvarying self-satisfaction. When a nation is not a state but an extended community, its emblems are altogether more varied and diffuse. They express not so much certainties as wishful thoughts and longings, or touchstones to hang on to. They represent values, ideas, inherited memories, objects that are familiar to the whole community, just as in the home a sepia photograph of a great-grandfather or an heirloom taken to Patagonia serves to link the generations of a family, and with luck give some cohesion to its relationships.

Even so, even in a country like Wales, they can go very sour. On the one hand they can be distorted into patriotic excess. The good old Welsh dragon can be made to seem as arrogant as the two-headed eagle of the Hapsburgs, waved in the hands of those who see Welsh nationhood as something narrow and intolerant. The emblems of the south can be used in bitter prejudice against those of the north – and vice versa. Sporting passions can be almost as ugly here as they are anywhere, and even Wales, with its three million people of mixed origins, can unwittingly use its familiar icons to try and prove itself more special than anywhere else.

Worse still, perhaps, those icons can be degraded for commerce. How preposterously the red dragon has been distorted in trademarks and posters, comically twisted and caricatured on travel brochures and T-shirts! The more familiar an icon is, the more tastelessly it is exploited by the tourist industry, until even the most charming or moving manifestations of public life are vulgarised. Antique hats, strange words, mountain ponies, rugby players, sweet Welsh rain, Eisteddfodau, bards, mines, harpers, Celtic Heritage and chapel piety – nothing is beyond the cheap touch of the publicist or the uncomprehending stare of the visitor. So icons, even in their modern meaning, can be good as well as bad. They can exalt or they can demean, they can give hope and comfort to a community or they can incite it to false claims.

The grandest and on the whole the best of Welsh icons is Wales itself, a tough, durable and fascinating place. But it is no more than a distillation of all the lesser emblems, familiar to all Welsh people – sometimes all too familiar – which David Greenslade has identified and interpreted in this book. His is an iconostasis warm, wise and often funny, its music the sound of poetry, rugby crowds, children playing and male voice choirs, its light coming not from candles but from daffodils and safety lamps, its colours scarlets, greys and rainy blues, with horses and greyhounds around it, small beer spilled on the floor and a souvenir tea-towel hanging over a prayer-mat.

Jan Morris

Leek

The leek is a member of the onion family and as such traces its origins to that period when the Egyptian Empire brought back bears from the cedar forests of Lebanon and onions from the Atlas Mountains. From Egypt the onion travelled via Celtic diplomats, evolving in colder alpine gardens into a hardy forerunner of the modern Welsh onion or leek. This much history of Wales' national vegetable is given in Pliny's Historia Naturalis. The leek became associated with the patron saint of Wales via a series of hagiographic profiles collected by copyists during the Middle Ages. Rhygyfarch tells us that St David used the very short rootlets of the leek to illustrate the minimal worldly needs of those satellite cells his followers were building in Brittany and Cornwall. But even the freshest leek will quickly deteriorate once the base of its root is cut away. The leek, being almost entirely stem, became associated with the ascetic practice of the Saint – specifically that of baptism and penance in rivers at all times of the year. Plucked from the field by marching soldiers, the leek easily adapted to patriotic horseplay and, before it was eaten by schoolboys, was eaten by Welsh mercenaries fighting for the Dutch. The Dutch expression for 'double Dutch' translates as 'gutter Welsh' and is a corruption of comments made when the impact of raw leeks made itself known in the barracks.

Welsh Hat

When the felt hat industry collapsed after the Crimean War and with the new availability of Georgian silk, hatmakers from Llangynfelyn, Ceredigion, emigrated to the Welsh settlements in Saskatchewan where, faced with different problems, they became engineers. Constructing the unlikely tall felt hat gave them a mathematical aptitude for quickly building strong wooden bridges over the many small rivers of the Canadian tundra. Permafrost and prairie replacing familiar felt, wax and resin. Frostbite attacking the skin instead of mercuric nitrate which, during hatmakers' carroting, would leech from the fleece into their sleeves and eventually get into their soup and drinking water – and so drive the careless hatter mad. The most famous Welsh hat is probably that worn by Mother Goose. A gypsy tale collected by George Borrow tells how one day Mother Goose's hat is knocked from her head when she passes underneath a rhubarb leaf. Four snakes emerge from the upturned hat – one red, one blue, one yellow and one white. Mother Goose goes with the white snake to Pwll y Pedair, one of the upland bogs of northern Ceredigion, where she carries a boy and girl across the *pwll* to safety. The children return the hat to Mother Goose and find that it is filled with buttons made of rubies and pearls.

Welsh Lady

Even though she has a name – Siân Owen – Vosper's Welsh Lady is really a portrait of a fabricated type – an anonymous bucolic throwback, a generic Jennie Jenkins, entirely worthy of being duplicated on a million Edwardian soap adverts and biscuit tins. She deserves to be pressed out on so many brass wall plates, drinking tea and eating *bara brith* next to her ever idle spinning wheel. More remarkable is that we regard her with affection as though we owe this particular image our respect. It resembles the irrepressible impulse some people have of sending cards and toys to the imaginary new-born babies of their favourite soap opera mums. Who can blame them? As for seeing the Devil in Siân Owen's shawl, this amounts to another form of essential veneration, like those games of boredom played among enlisted ranks such as folding a ten-pound note until the Queen's chin magically becomes a bald man's head; or a blue tattoo trick revealing all when thigh and calf are folded tight together. That this figure may be no lady needn't bother us – was she ever thus obliged? After all, Caradoc Evans was her nephew and, after paying homage, told us what it was her sister roasted when she sat at home, singing *'Calon Lân'*, dreaming of Welsh Rarebit late at night.

Dragon

The Dragon is fictitious the same way that dreams are fictitious, which they are not. It is in this sense that the Dragon appears on the military insignia of Welsh regiments. The Dragon signifies some erotic violence that cannot be easily communicated except via the sign itself; locked in the superfold of a fluttering banner. We know those cave-like depths where dragons sleep, brooding on a hoard of stolen wealth, when reptilian stirrings move us in unexpected ways – we are suddenly violent, infatuated, jealous, greedy, virile, invincible, immortal. It was St George himself who lost when, in his dream, he believed his lance had killed the Dragon. The English have never recovered from this act of erotic damage. So it is at British universities that Welsh students enjoy the reputation of being accomplished lovers. But, because of dragons, the Welsh often remain reckless and fixated, and both Richard Burton and Dylan Thomas experienced the horror of falling toward the Dragon's open throat. The Dragon lacks all sense of strategy, which is why the Welsh Rugby Union will never succeed in marketing 'the Dragons' as a nickname for the national side. To be close to the Dragon is to be close to an extreme condition – so that the Dragon must be far away, not with Arthur, but even further, located among the Libyan spoils of Vortigern. St George's Day will only be remembered as a popular holiday when that long lance learns to prick the reptiles of this world and not delude itself that it can kill them.

LLANDILO
SECONDS

Rugby

Whether it developed from those games of Cnapan in Llangyfelach reported by Iolo Morganwg, where the goals were eight miles apart and up to two thousand players were involved; or whether it evolved from those savage games where English public schools could not agree on rules, may never definitely be known. But the shape of the ball became quickly confirmed. It would be elliptical and not round. The same bull's bladder confined, not by a sphere of belts but by a leather torpedo of symmetrical tongues. A new ball for a new game. One of the first police rugby teams was formed in Swansea and its first fixture, in 1891, was against a team of Swansea Butchers. The Butchers paraded a bull before the game, which was slaughtered, its cooked meat sold after the game and the bladder washed and treated and made into a sort of ball which was presented to the winning side. Swansea Police won by scoring three tries – that is, by grounding the leather-wrapped bull's bladder across the line at the furthest end of their opponents' territory. The Butchers' tries were minored – which is to say nulled – because hands from both sides were touching the bladder as it found the ground. The custom of braying or bellowing, a hangover from Cnapan yodelling, was discouraged at rugby matches. It was felt that bellowing contributed to 'riotous behaviour' and to an increase in crime. Police rugby teams were, at first, difficult to justify because of rugby supporters' almost Mithraic appetite for crime and transgression.

Cardiff Arms Park

Perhaps the new stadium should be called Fisher King Arena – since just as the Fisher King's dolorous wound matched the devastation of the country, so the condition of Wales' 'national' sport directly affects the mood of many of its people. Popular clichés spoken in the rugby clubs change with fortunes of the game. 'Superb' when thumbs are up. 'Shattered' when they are down. 'Too royal' when all agree. 'Up yours' at times of commissariat conflict. In her study 'Sexuality in the South Wales Rugby Clubs', Dr Charlotte Green records how, during demolition of the former Arms Park Stadium, the institution of the weekly rugby club disco degenerated into scenes of violent and unusual promiscuity and, in one instance, a case of kidnap and rape. Arms Park was named after a nearby munitions factory staffed mainly by women devoted to the military salvation of the British Isles at a time of national emergency. Or was it, after all, just a nearby pub? Suggested names for the new stadium included Public Utility Millennium Stadium and Stadium of the Heroes of Rugby Administration. There are many schoolboys who don't know what is played there.

Harp

The earliest Celtic harps, recorded by Strabo, were aeolian or wind harps. These harps were sophisticated instruments and consisted of wires made from tin, copper or gold pulled between the branches and trunks of oak trees. They could also be made of waxed thread, tarred flax or animal gut. These wires whistled or hummed as they cut the wind that blew across them. The harp itself, as a semi-plucked, semi-percussive instrument, is as old as Western civilisation. Its mythical European origins go back to the birth of Hermes and his slaughter of a tortoise, from which the frame of the first harp or lyre was made. The modern Welsh or triple harp is an instrument of such unusual precision and tension that stress exercised by the strings between the neck and pedestal via the pillar is equivalent, in engineering terms, to the torsion of the entire Second Severn Crossing, which succeeds through an inversion of load-bearing stress over three and a half miles, as opposed to an intensification of stress within five feet. Unlike the classical orchestra harp, the Welsh triple harp is customarily played on the left shoulder.

Tiger Bay

Being there is like being at the top of a hundred-foot pole. A place you can't claim until you've distanced yourself from it – or have never been there. And now that it doesn't exist any more, the long canal drained, railway closed and the deep docks trimmed with expensive maisonettes, it's safer still. As fetid as any port in the world and as rich a stew as the best and the worst. Famous. Kowloon, San Francisco, Bombay, Liverpool, Tiger Bay – all in the same breath. And a family could be fetched up, bankrupt or just as easily saved at any one of them. Riches of the Nile land washed by floods of arriving people, their cells and sayings among mangles of every description. The Flesh of the world confined beyond the Great Western Railway, not far from Cardiff Gaol, away from Ivor Novello and the genteel city. The Afro-Celtic block, named by the Portuguese, straightlaced by Yemeni ghat, scented with Greek olive oil and a byword for all projections of riches and descent. This square mile was the body, the stoker, the last Nurse and Mother between Merthyr and the international engine room. There's no insulting the capital of backchat and Cardiff calypso, no lower turn of phrase. Demolished in the clean sweep of the 1960s when its M.P. knew the value of strike-bound property. Where once it was vigorously checked, Old Tiger Bay is now open country in the heritage industry's glossy mind.

Buried City

Scratch between Port Talbot and Porthcawl and you'll find a buried city. That fertile, sandy, rail-crossed triangle of land, best viewed from Ton Farm near the hamlet of Tai Thorn, conceals buried secrets – from well offerings at Ffynnon Fawr in Nottage and the broken heart at Sger to early Cistercian coal workings at Groes and isolated hermit cells drowned beneath Eglwys Nynnid. Between them, the buried castle of the ancient City of Kenfig just visible from the motorway, beyond the Orion micro-circuits factory. Buried disappointments beneath the skin – each *cantre gwaelod* at the bottom of a pint of Brains – what are they good for? They make the unemployed discrete – walking the railway line with a length of rope. You see a hand sticking up and tie a knot around it. It could be Arthur! The sleeping king! Or it might be why you lost your job, why you're living in a flat in North Cornelly on your own. Why, every night, you sit at home getting drunk on home-brew and stoned on home-grown bush. Buried cities beneath the skin. Riches we don't recognise. Perhaps we shouldn't go into it.

Hills

There have been many attempts to make mountains out of Welsh hills. *I Bought a Mountain, Taking Tiger Mountain by Storm, The Man Who Went up a Hill and Came Down a Mountain* – to list only a few of the most recent. But the hill is far from commonplace and being among their folds probably answers a need that has long affected the British race. Cambrian hills consist mainly of Pleistocene compressed igneous grits, with, in the north and south, some radically fractured seams of carboniferous slate and coal. Welsh hills generally bald and fertile, are far from Alps but the terminology of hills, (like the terminology of colours), in Welsh, translates well into Swiss German – confirming some roots and branches of the Welsh language. It is well known that hills 'boom' or call to listeners and that they boom less often for the busy. The Black Hills of South Dakota boomed loudly both to migrants and the native population until the 1920s. But, since the tragedy of gold opencast mining at Homestake, they now boom only to individuals and no longer for the whole community. Wales has several clusters of hills that occasionally boom, and these sounds are sometimes reported with alarm. But the only booming that is still being regularly heard by entire villages is between the most eastern Preselis and southern Plumlumons, north of Cwmfelin Mynach. There is no scientific explanation for these extended rumbling sounds which resemble more of a groaning or purring than any kind of explosion.

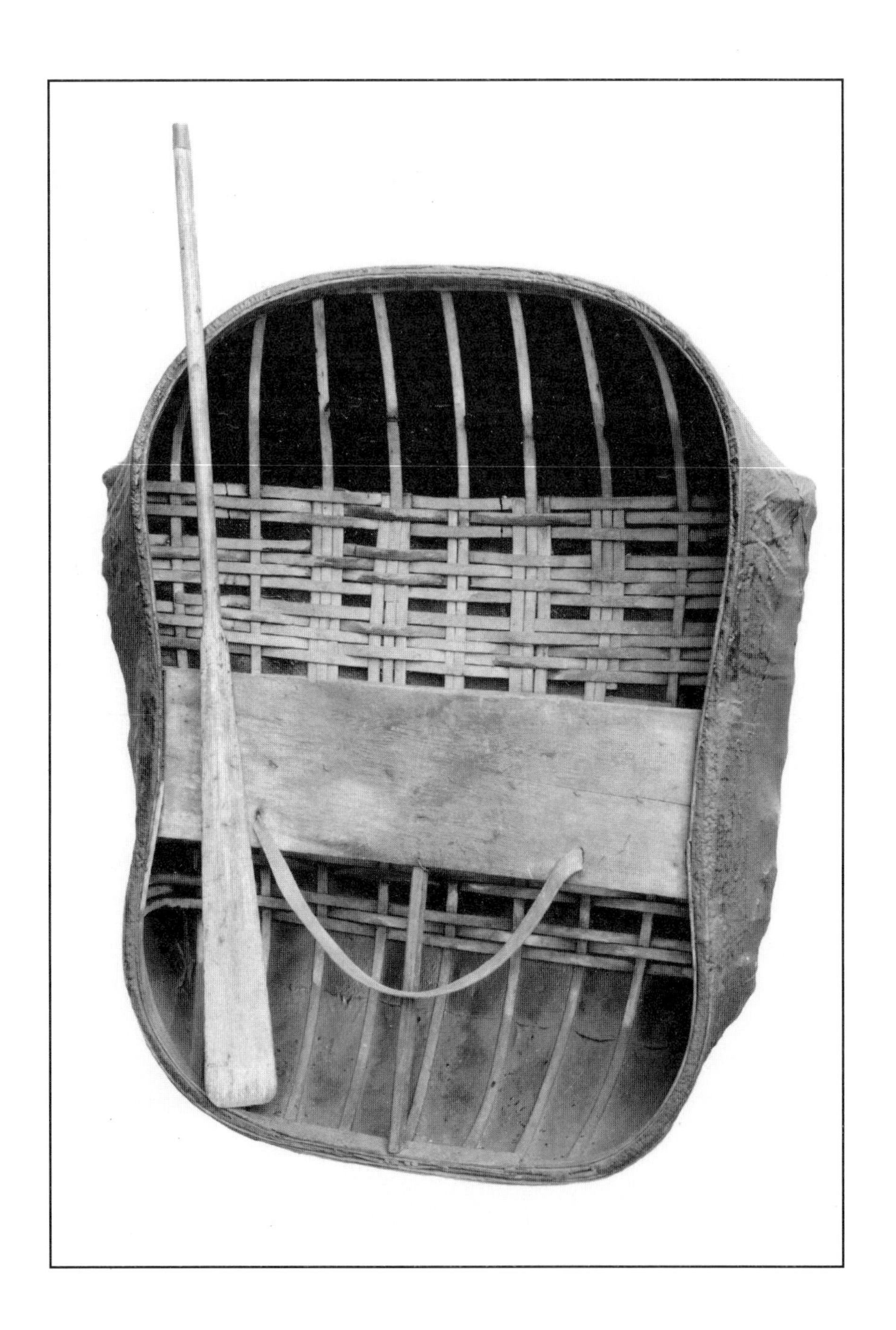

Coracle

These corks bobbing to Iceland from Cenarth – some from the Teifi found Canada. Drifting westward with just a little salt and bread, water dissolving and absolving the isolated anchorite from the coagulations of social devotion. Ocean and freshwater coracle going intentionally shallow-draught and rudderless, plaited strong enough to cast the hermit free of land. For a fasting hairshirt bound for heaven, fire and rock were a cruel surprise. Stunned like a salmon gasping in the net's wrong threshold. Dry in a willow pigskin dish. Today calico and pitch, bob, bob, bobbing along licensed banks of real estate. Bluntest kayak hunting with the clearest abandoned purpose. Prayer that one impetuous stroke would spin into the longest *chwyrndrobwllpwllgwyngyll* not to a keepered stream but one, corpse cast, that got away. Unless God's club spared the crib and all dilemmas miraculous. Prepared by study, craft has government – dry as a leaf, managing currents by accident.

Sheep

The sheep in Wales serves as a kind of Rorschach inkblot test. Projections at it are frequently tasteless and often therapeutic. If you share the same prurient humour as the Lord Mayor of Cardiff [then, Timothy H. Davies, Labour] when he spoke to an elderly, hymn-singing, genteel and sophisticated after dinner audience at the National Cymanfa Ganu in the Hilton Hotel Grand Ballroom in Harrisburg, the capital city of Pennsylvania, then you should make every effort to see the photograph Bob Leet and His Sheep by Arthur Tress. Bob Leet and his sheep are both naked. Once established it is difficult to escape this kind of tone and, indeed, his Worship the Right Honourable Lord Mayor of Cardiff, disgraced his city and was heckled. Those sheep! You don't have to imagine molesting them.

Sheep Dog

Useless out of the field, a decoy flapping from the nest, a pair of wings trying to stick themselves on hostile wellingtons. All black and belly white, legs giving way, legs looser than the tail; head lolling like a skittle, rolling like a plastic pop bottle knocked between road and pavement. Dribbling, panting, squeaking like a toy duck. Helplessly alert. The sheepdog bitch is safer, and we're relieved when she's back in the dark of the jeep. At work, her jaw as close as sandpaper through the field's steep grass; and, like water, *gloyw-loyw*, flowing from side to side at the pebbly heels of sheep. A whoa! constrictor swallowing all the flock into one stone corner. As a flame is firm, like a jet of steam, she's firm at the fleecy meat. And, in early spring – when placenta beach like jellyfish – having laboured all winter in the accurate whistle's leading left and curving right, she and her young cousin share the still warm body of a stillborn mountain lamb. Useless pet. She never wins indoors. She earns Tyddynnwr's poem, a litter of silver cups glittering on the cluttered mantleshelf.

Corgi

Corgis were originally bred by Flemish weavers as rat catchers. They were also used by the earliest drovers as cattle 'heelers' when they moved their stock along the Drovers' Roads. The Corgi is considered to be one of the more intelligent canine breeds and, at Crufts as well as finals of the Westminster Kennel Club, has frequently taken first and other top prizes in the Steeplechase Hunting and Herding field trial category – beating the Border Collie and the Alsatian German Shepherd dog. The English Monarch has kept Corgis since George VI was made a present of them from Rozavel Kennels and the first royal dog 'Golden Eagle' bred with 'Lady Jane'. The two main pedigree types today are the Cardigan Corgi and the formerly unrelated Pembroke Corgi. The Pembroke being shorter and with specified colours – sable, red, black, tan, also bred without a tail; the Cardigan enjoying freer colours – among them, golden orange, brindled and even bright fox-red. It is believed that the first modern Pembroke Corgi was bred by Twm Sion Cati when a tailless dog of his ('descended of a Viking hounde') mated with a vixen. These pups later bred with other tailless dogs which the outlaw, following his pardon in 1559, brought with him from Estonia into the Tregaron district.

Greyhound

Up North, the whippet. In Maerdy, Neath and Annwfn – the greyhound. The best greyhounds rarely see the light of day – released at night, their red-tipped ears race along the incline, when it's so quiet you can hear the mushrooms grow. The thin town far below and the dog's elongated heart beating louder than the small shunter and its slow train of long containers coming off the marshalling yard. Frisbee-fresh, the greyhounds both come back – shoulders and moth-soft paw-fall eaten up in the wet vicarious appetite of being that swift falcon meat on four paradiddle drumsticks. And in the stadium floodlight, ribbons and fluorescent numbers – now they are tortoiseshell, now they are brown or grey – lice-heavy pigeons too liable to lose. Suddenly driven from perfect admiration into a competitive rack of bays. They let us down even when they win – needing towels, a biscuit, a brace on one weak leg, authorised documents. Their etiolated counterparts run to the ford on other limbs, while these, slobbering and hungry, admit their limits, limp into the ragged boot, creep into their buckled cage.

Male Voice Choir

One hundred and twenty men who, when they walk on stage, make less noise than a frog spawning fry at the edge of a small pond. It's a conceit that's easily continued. White shirts over Sunday bellies, dark ties like embryonic threads. Frogs! And when they sing, rain falls! Small dots of it through the catchments of their songsheets. Maroon blazers, matching ringbinders like colour tv testcards sanitising the concert into an overfamiliar repertoire. Later, away from stage, there's prizegiving and dinners. A visitor who doesn't know better tries to get a sing-song going in the lobby of the conference hotel. But the uniformed choristers, contracted to their rehearsals, prefer to talk and prefer to have a pint. Strangely quiet, mutually obedient, their respiratory pauses vacuuming the concert hall long after they have filed, by groups – each assigned according to late night habits – towards each particular designated bus.

The Valleys

All yin and not much chance, without serious upheaval, of getting a glimpse of geographic yang – only what people bring in their pockets by bus, train, lorry, van, motorbike, ambulance, bike, roller-skate, police helicopter, by foot and by car. Back and fore – to work, to the butcher's, the chemist's, further down for groceries and petrol. There's not much side to side. At night, drunk, the stars end half way through Orion's Belt, the Great Bear dips into the solid dark and Venus plants her kiss on curving ferns. To the south, a little space, but why desire there and all its open clanging? Here, as the paintings of Ernest Zobole, Iwan Bala and Josef Herman show, the yin nest has its pipes of gas and beer, electricity and morphine. Here the streets curl like cabled wool close to their tubes of need. Anything bigger than a shed crushed by something called a 'market force'. In the morning, when the lights come on – some houses coiled as tight as Catherine wheels, others singing to the day in memory of Ann. She raved here.

Cymanfa Ganu

Ieuan Gwyllt (John Roberts, 1822-1877), the original voice movement therapist. Song and inner body awareness – community ecstasy emerging from homes with barns but without bathrooms, from open fields, from the figure of the first frock-coated, isolated leader with no tradition standing behind him. He invented it – the *Cymanfa Ganu* (literally, singing assembly) in Aberdare, 1859. Tonic sol-fa bubbling up like Persian oil into a jubilee of descants, echoes, harmonies, widenings, repeats and improvisations. Restrained and encouraged by the great Nonconformist urge to prove themselves capable of building untrained choral cathedrals. Plural:– *cymanfaoedd canu* – held in Alaska and the Yukon. Jack London in his story Seaborne Jones's Journey tells the yarn of a slightly built, tough, pugilistic, Welsh silver miner confounding his cynical partners by making the trip from Dawson to Skagway, then on to Seattle to attend the 1909 Alaska Yukon Territorial *Cymanfa* and how he found a wife there. Later distorted into a film starring Stewart Granger. The great Welsh American *Cymanfa Ganu* started as a Youngstown steelworkers' picnic in 1929. Anyone who has ever been to this event will have experienced the wild energy of voice in a basically conservative environment. Fancy hotels, ID lapel badges, the protocol of blue collar denominationalism. Few sleep; fewer fail to fall in love and fewer still fail to be deeply moved by the community benediction when 'old country' hymns are finally finished. Folded like sacramental garments back into closets of the *'gwasgaredig'* tongue.

Safety Lamp

Surrounded by water on three sides, enjoying fresh Atlantic air and rich, at all levels through the soil, Wales also has its share of notable fire. Two fires, which were never extinguished, spring immediately to mind – Senghennydd and the Fire in Llŷn. There are others, and they are never far away, as the list of Colliery Disasters reminds us. Terrorist fire has never really taken hold in Wales despite the enthusiasm of M.A.C. or arson raids on holiday homes by the British Secret Service. That these particular fires still burn in other parts of the British Isles is a legacy of Margaret Thatcher's violent assault on the notion of community and is not unique to Wales. Here, Cornishman Sir Humphry Davy's Safety Lamp – also claimed by Stephenson – has become a heritage souvenir. Heavy iron gauze and concave glass keep the small, well-nourished flame from igniting the combustible population. Subterranean passages filled with the crushed decay of forest oils and tars. A primitive sponge of unyielding fuel – difficult to start and difficult to extinguish. What is this allegorical gauze that keeps so many people asking what were the Blue Books? Who was Saunders Lewis? Bilingualism.

Coal

The trouble is, although they are dressed up, these three little boys are not wearing dress-up clothes. In this photograph I am five, my brother is four. David Lloyd, who lived next door, is also five. My father was a face worker at Pentre, later at Newlands colliery but David's father, 'Whisky' Lloyd, drove a lorry. 'Whisky' drove a lorry until he keeled over and died on the pavement after a heavy afternoon in the Three Horse Shoes. My father was a collier until he broke his neck against the lash of a haulier's chain. Our trousers are tied below the knee just in case the wind running through the galleries chose our particular dress-up legs as its rat hole. The size of the head doesn't change that much (which always fascinated my father) and we wear real miners' helmets. The knapsacks, real miners' knapsacks used in Newlands. The coal on our faces taken from lumps and small, tipped on the road at the top of our steps. But we were dress-up miners. Dress-up. Because, whenever we saw him at teatime, his mouth full of bacon and egg, my father used to shout at us, 'You won't go down the bloody mine. You won't go down the bloody mine.' And when his back had healed after a year at Tal-y-garn, from the time I was nine and my brother was eight years old, he worked seven days a week to stop us dressing up like him. His grandfathers were farm labourers from Somerset. His father died of pneumoconiosis. 'You won't go down the bloody mine.'

Welsh Pit Disaster. A little mother waiting for news.

Pit Head Wheel

The pit head wheel is big – was big – was never big enough. Could never haul enough out, nor drop enough down into its self-enfolding labyrinth. As well as men and ponies, gear, slag and coal, the regal pit head wheel served as a librarian's helper, lowering H.G. Wells' and J.B. Priestley's books to generations of south Wales colliers. And those legendary manuscripts they passed from hand to hand! – all hauled out when the big wheel turned and the colliery had to close. Corpses too, whole or in several parts, told their story when the big wheel turned. The blanket across one shoulder, passed beneath one arm, tightened momentarily when the wheel brought up its forklift palette of television sets. Near the wheel, the river – now clear, now red – passing by the outhouse of the panel-beater's garage. The wheel makes a pale blue apple tart of the fluffy Sunday sky. The wheel that made a mess of things.

How Green Was My Valley

How easily it suits us to project our exploitation upon another age. Rape of the Fair Country, building the barrage at Cardiff Bay, dotting the coast with postcard picturesque marinas. Then the narrator was an invalid boy, one of those engulfed at Aberfan. It's easier to build a *Drych* to the *Prif Oesoedd* than reflect upon the current period – species disappearing, radioactive suds at Langland Bay, award-winning slums at the Penrhys Virgin's Well, forced migration into rural Wales of the English urban unemployed. Once a new beginning meant Off to Philadelphia in the Morning. Now what? A seat in the House of Lords? Eventually someone writes a book called *The Welsh Extremist*, followed twenty years later by fly posters calling for the release of the Cyfamodwyr Four. The miner, meanwhile, hasn't quite become the Rob Roy or leprechaun of the heritage industry – but not through lack of trying. When Maerdy went as Little Moscow the imperial police marched in. Today heritage centres carry lucrative picture books of bygone hardships. Deeply undermined, dumped on, riddled by buckling galleries, the geological content of the Rhondda now fits in an exhibition case; dressed up tour guides also unpersuaded that they ever had it so good.

The River Taff

Compared with Yank or Frog, Jock or Sassenach, it's an honour to be nicknamed after Yahweh's harpist *and* a British river. If it were dirtier with the hopes of bliss-determined human ashes then the nickname 'Taff'– clipped from the dark waters of Dafydd – would be even richer. As it is the river is merely littered with the indifferent despair of cars, wrappers, mattresses and supermarket trolleys. Despite municipal money and a post-coal clean-up the Taff remains a local gutter, the principal phobic demon of the Cardiff Bay Development Corporation, the back-end enema of allotments from Grangetown to Cefncoedycymer where it splits like a lopsided serpent's tongue. At Blackweir school children venture down the banks to swim in it. Ducks and sewin adjusting to its poison. Where the Taff Fawr rises from its sump at Dolygaer there's an English-only 'Mountain Centre' and at Rhydfelen, site of the first Welsh-medium comprehensive school in Glamorgan, cul-de-sacs named after Byron, Tennyson, Coleridge and Wordsworth. These names adopted by the same councillors who wanted to rename Ynysangharad Park because it was difficult to pronounce. Taff – let's hire a dancer, get drunk, conspire in a corporate entertainment suite and deny the crap that's still flowing into it.

Slate

Chilblains: although generally known as 'burning snow' *(llosgeira)*, one local word for this affliction could be translated as snow-slate or snow-stone – *llecheira*. It's well-known how chilblains bring snow on. Perhaps these inflammatory, itchy devils earned their bond with slate the same way that mug handles earned their link with *dolen*; or the way that some swollen abutments and appendages earn their compound with *clust* (ear) like *pwll* or *llech*, other almost infinitely compliant nouns. Infinitely servile, like that prize raised monkey-rump *Llanfairpwllgwyngyllgogerychwyrndrobwllllantysiliogogogoch*. Slates are more difficultly pliable. As commodious as good knitting. But the further they went the thinner they became. So that slate flatly contradicts that insidious proverb *Gorau Cymro, Cymro oddi cartref*. Thinner and thinner. Until the strikers are singing 'Myfanwy' in the snow with only their chilblains on. Blue like ghosts, rattling with the tap-tap-tap of lock-out, tally and confiscated tools. When the roof is stripped, broken proverbs blow out through the rafters and the slates are on their way. Away from home, pillaged and not inclined to reminisce, the hole in which they squatted harder than any peach bottom.

Rain

When it rains the kids go bonkers and a school in Wales becomes an unpredictable place to be. Wind and heavy drizzle open little lock gates in their cells until they're running up and down the corridors committing ritual acts of sport in the labyrinthine dodge of keeping dry. But they don't keep dry. The boys throw down their school bags in the pools. Girls flick long wet hair out from behind the doors. They kick at broken gutters. Gouge up the grassy banks. Whip it off the teachers' cars. Stand heads back, mouths wide open, yelling in delight when some good size drops fall in. They 'accidentally' drop their books in it. Stamp it. Swear at it. Fling their faces in bushes brimming with it. They love it and they hate it. Insist on dragging it into the classroom. They gleam with it. They are birds in it. They are buffalo. They are children in it – disruptive, heedless in wet baptismal plenty pouring endlessly onto their hair, foreheads, noses, shoulders – their truant dives, their paths to school, their shimmering yards and playing fields. They go mad in it. They stink, they squeal, they complain, they shiver and they cry. Unrestrained – elbowing school aside, getting their direct transmission, their education from the RAIN.

GWIR YN ERBYN
BYD

Crown

For certain, it's not a hat, but the winning poet imagines wearing it whenever the *testunau* forecast another walk with words. Warm applause, cutting like a fountain pen, binds the crown to the annual glue of ritual sponsorship, searchlight response and commissioned regalia. It's a lunar bonnet more than a solar tiara. Outrageous and ornate in 1880, but simplified, after Dolgellau 1933, into an authentic if ultimately nominal cap. A hoop for the lyricist to leap through, with a magic bag at the end – now for Gwawl, now for Rhiannon – to disappear into. Crowns are treated like individuals but with regal honour. Being a crown, its feet cannot touch the ground, and woven for the head it too, as dreams are, is carried by embroidered pillow. But this dream means there is no separation from the darker side of triumph. Faced by auditorium lights – and beyond them, one fifth in statistical obscurity, the uncrowned heads of those who live by other dreams – the crowned poet is seared to the present. Awake to the victory that poetry's subterranean paths have cleared. Unlike military medals, these prizes never fall onto the open market. What happens to them? Like elephants, they find their way back into the *testunau* from which they came.

Bardic Chair

Following the controversy between Ieuan Glan Geirionydd (Evan Evans, Trefriw) and Caledfryn (William Williams, Bryn y Ffynnon) by 1860 it was decided that the annual National Eisteddfod Crown should be awarded for the winning *pryddest* and the National Eisteddfod Chair for the winning *awdl*, that is for writing completed in a variety of the twenty-four established measures of alliterative and assonantal *cynghanedd*. Some chairs are more famous than others. Some, with more ornamentation than a Swansea Market souvenir stand, were justly ridiculed by Cynan for their Atlas complex – for trying to locate the whole Welsh cosmos around one winning poet's backside. Others, such as the Black Chair of Birkenhead, spontaneously emerging as a genuine national symbol, a reflection of the relationship between poets, who were often nothing more than Montezuma's Magicians, and the British State. The Shanghai Chair, won by David James Jones in 1926, is at another extreme. Sitting in it, completely at ease in carpet slippers, Gwenallt looks more like a stoker at the Mond than an Aberystwyth academic. These days the design of the Chair owes a lot to the work of Charles Rennie Mackintosh, who liberated 'Celtic' design from knotwork and menhirs. At least the modern chair will fit in the winner's home. Nowadays, even poets can afford their furniture – and the chair doesn't have to dominate the house as though it were an object of Messianic veneration.

Stone Circle

Diogenes the Cynic heard of them. While living 'like a dog' in a tub, Diogenes may have been the first to idealise the Druids and their Temples in the open air. That long ago, *Côr y Cewri* was already old and the word Stone-henge for it uncoined. Carnac sinking away from perfect lines. Some of those who live in Wales still raise their voices out of circles of stone. The last civic stone circle being erected at Tredegar House for the Newport Eisteddfod in 1988. As a civic ritual, construction has been delegated to a JCB and a gang of men in donkey jackets. It has been left to those outside British constitutional law to maintain this human connection with Hyperborean happiness. D. Tecwyn Lloyd in particular loved, with solemnity and with practical jokes, to stand on the Maen Llog or 'announcement stone' of the Gorsedd Circle. International rugby player Ray Gravell cut short a tour overseas in order to be an aide at the Ogwr Gorsedd Circle *cyhoeddiad*. Elected politicians stayed away. After all, ritual is absurd – insisting that all secular intent be suspended for a session of ceremonial play. Witness to a world that is always shoddy and undignified. All the more reason to stand on a piece of rock and praise it.

Bard

The druidic bard, who could imagine him failing to be virile? It's unthinkable. His enormous shoulders, Popeye the Sailorman forearms, limitless eloquence, furious eyes, kind mouth, hair – long, white, windblown, dandruff free; and his toga, where did he get it? It's a profession that allows the best tea tree shampoos and frequent foreign holidays. He wears plaited bands of pure gold, money torcs; sometimes a broad collar across his breast and when he's out he carries a nifty sceptre. Invented after being slaughtered. A scholar whose ogam knowledge notched the stars, whose language named the weapons and the weeds of Gaul. Today, honoured in California and ridiculed in Cardiff. Ridiculed until a blue or green or white invitation to become one falls through the letterbox. And then how quickly slippery Iolo gets forgiven. Caesar explained. There are few as relaxed as an Archdruid and no one better qualified to put a Crown on a poet's head, or place their hand on the shoulder of a poet who has won the Chair. When he does this, the Archdruid publicly praises the winning poet, both at an intimate and ceremonial level. The exchange is spontaneous and completely public. The Archdruid both calms and elevates the need of his people to hear the hearth of their language burn.

Dwynwen

She is a small corrugated seashell opening her valves in the tidal shallows of a deep bay at the edge of an enormous salty heart. When she calls you'll hear it and if you don't turn all your waves to her, you're dead. All layers of love are hers, from care of family and gardens to irreversible acts of obsessive stupidity. Living with her requires skill, courage and devotion. She can be a wife at every stolen step; a maid following every wasted footprint. Fish, untrained and untrainable, redeem what was lost, hurled from her in sorrow or in rage to the very edge of the world. She can reach even as far as you, remote and hard-hearted, having turned your back on the primitive romance that made you. When it is cold and absolutely clear how much was lost, how suddenly the forested land is merely just so many acres in an annual report, the time you lived there opportunist merit points towards divorce, you might long for something you knew would never come again. Her comfort is beneath your dignity – lowering your kiss towards a scallop; her foamy bubbles forming on your tongue, her inferior phrases limping from your learner's lips.

DAPPERS

Eisteddfod Plate

The visiting soprano looked a little concerned. Her overseas host was showing her their Eisteddfod Plate, with which he was clearly delighted. Also the Eisteddfod Plastic Bag with similar motifs. They would be given away free with Eisteddfod Market Place merchandise. As well as singing, the distinguished, prize-winning visitor would also be Mistress of Ceremonies. But things weren't quite as she thought they should be and she had trouble getting started. She took a deep breath. Your plate is certainly different. You like it? I've never seen anything like it. It's an original concept and we're very pleased. I don't quite understand some of the connections. Well there's Mighty Moth, honouring the Island of the Mighty. Fishnet stockings honouring the Goddesses of the Mabinogion. The flamingo is a tribute to the bird lore of our ancient bards. And the pistol? Rorke's Drift. The syringe? Contemporary life. A blue marlin? *Yma o Hyd.* She shook her head and smiled at that one. You're serious, aren't you? Thank you, he replied. We've done a lot of research. We were hoping you'd be pleased.

Teapot

Tea is first mentioned in a Chinese document by Lo Yu in 780 AD. Tea drinking in Wales became a national habit a thousand years later when British colonists in India discovered a way of drying tea leaves quickly enough so that they would yield their taste when hot water was added. The European market grew from this important step. As well as discovering a link between Sanskrit, Old Persian and the Celtic languages, High Court Judge in Bengal, *Cymmrodor* Sir William 'Oriental' Jones, wrote articles advising readers in Wales that dried tea leaves brewed in iron and copper pots made a bitter and less palatable drink compared with tea brewed in china, porcelain or even earthenware. Early European china teapots, with spout, lid and handle – teapots that we would recognise today – were made in south Wales potteries both in Swansea and at Nantgarw, to the north of Cardiff along the River Taff. The teapot spout – being part of a closed container and liable to get quickly clogged – proved to be a challenge, and, since Chinese and Japanese bulbed examples were rare, Welsh designers experimented with many often impractical widths and shapes before the right proportions were found. Eventually Welsh china teapots were sold in India and 'Spout' became a common nickname of 'packmen' between the Tawe, Taff and the Brahmaputra.

Welsh Dresser

This is where the upland farmer, working in a gap among the clouds, sets the suicide note that his daughter will later find. Where Freddie Welsh kept his perfumed fan letters from America. Where, between the pewter jug and digital calendar, the union solicitor keeps his four-wheel-drive keys. Waxed by six generations of the same family's hands, until it's almost as red and as lively as the wood from which the distant sawyer cut it, the dresser slowly buckles until it resembles an immediate relative. In Tondu, Maesteg and Bettws there are homes still boasting dressers that Wil Hopkin made, before he moved to Bristol and made Welsh dressers there. The dresser drawers, floating in a deep iodine embrace, filled with teatowels, pencils, fountain pens, cheques, a spare radiator key, a prescription for tablets and a coverless ready reckoner. Before the funeral a sister and a brother lift off the heavy crockery, take the top half down, remove the drawers and carry the cupboard to the middle of the room. The next day the coffin rests on it. A decade later, eating from the same blue-edged plates, a small boy gazes at an unfamiliar patch of kitchen wall framed between the dresser shelves.

WELSH
LOVE
SPOONS
WALES
WELSH
LANGUAGE

Tea Towel

Tactful, so tactful it's tactless and quickly we hate it – the heritage teatowel. Its selection of bridges, enlarged parts of the prettiest portions of the country, queer words, breeds, selected national costume. Made in Britain, a tactful way of avoiding having to say that it wasn't made in Cornwall, that it wasn't made in the Isle of Man. Like 'hand finished' or 'hand selected' or 'no added sugar', hardly the forum for challenging the nature of Language or the nature of Heritage itself, but why not? A ticket through Turner Country, Hardy Country, Cordell Country. Tickets through Carnuanhawc Country, Dave Datblygu Edwards Country are harder to get. Hunllef Arthur Country. Glass of wine in one hand, tea towel over the shoulder; Steiner School; an Observer's Guide to Nora Chadwick; measuring out one's holiday afternoon with reproductive lovespoons. It's a package deal and finally we buy a house there – finding that the hospital is staffed by people just like us, forced into a logical decision to close it down. Until it all makes sense and we deeply resent the two pounds seventy-five we spent on it.

Small Beer

Can small beer really take the blame for a culture of small ambitions? Third pressings. Wales and the West sales division with its sweeteners and tribute money to keep the regional edifice intact. Big enough so that white shirts, blazers and Labour Club ties can claim it all in the name of 'Sowth' Wales interests. Hardly the same as 'small is beautiful'. Cables lowering pilfered buckets of home-brew from the top of the world tree. At its bottom, rotten meat falling like love bites from the eagle's wing. Wren's piss in the Red Sea. In Search of Wales lost like a lentil among the thousand desperate tasks of marketing an image. Living off small and mash while the best steam coal goes piping through the Royal Navy. It isn't what gets mined, but the stodge and slag of conifer-infested lees that's left behind. The essential oil of Brecon therapists deciding the fate of Dowlais care and section policies. When the imagination must be new and nice, safe and lovely and too tidy to be used, like a gift that's easily chosen. Put in some cabinet where it looks as though someone really enjoyed this kind of novelty. Just because Mam or Dad lack the nerve to speak as some still speak in Croeserw and in Caerau. Listen love, couldn't you find a worser piece of tinsel than that to bring me? Stuff it – and your plastic gondola.

Lovespoon

The smallest lovespoon ever made was carved from a phosphorous taper or 'Stockton Lucifer' as the first commercially made matches were known. It was carved by a Mr Vaynor Jones of Tenby – lens grinder to the Pembrokeshire marine industry, lay preacher and a translator, into Welsh, of Spinoza's Essays on Rationalism. Vaynor Jones' lovespoon, which weighed less than one fiftieth of an apothecary's ounce, was displayed at Tenby Town Museum until a fire destroyed the building in 1822. But numerous drawings were made of the lovespoon and J.M.W. Turner describes it in his *Diaries of Wales* (1795). We know that this folk miniature featured the usual lovespoon repertoire of hearts, links, apostrophes (or soul signs), boxed spheres, a dolphin banister, the Tenby daffodil and initials of the carver's wife. Jones lived in a house previously owned by Robert Recorde, mathematician and inventor of the equals (=) sign. The largest lovespoon anyone has documented was cut by chainsaw from the trunk of a Portuguese oak at the Severn Revels Music Festival held in 1997 at Newnham Agricultural College, Forest of Dean. This carving, from green wood, featured links, boxed spheres and a four-foot long unsanded bowl.

Dawns Llangrannog

These not-mind feet, the sheer spark of their not-doing is exhilarating. Not grinding an axe, not paving the way, not compromising on a deal, not forging an identity. As safely and as sure-footed as angels dancing on a pin – they dance, in circles and in rows, in the gym. Dancing Llangrannog into the ground. Straining Nike and Clarkes, Adidas and Co-op – against jeans, sweat suits and voluminous, loose fitting clothing. Care cast away. The mirage of isolated separation, of being colonised, being told by others what they are – rumbled and undone in the vigour of their own unconditional display. These feet – where they return to terraces and bungalows; flats and estates – the Celtic Fringe, the bi-valve, the judge's mallet, the spongy mass. How will they decide? To rant, rave, leap, turn, dare, invent, devise, discover, flow, trust, search, lift, step, rush, go, commit, respond, notice, feel, hear, bend, roar, applaud, decide, love, show, open and embrace? How will they reflect on how once they beamed until noticing that they too were suddenly reflected? How? With a passport? With a wedding ring? With a job? There was a knot of energy, it broke from the gym, raiding the corridors, laughing at an open window. One polished moment of ineluctable delight. Torn from the outset towards erotic options. When they removed their dancing shoes. Laces tied or untied. Their dreaming tongues.

Red Kite

From six birds in 1900 to one hundred and six by the year 2000 – it took a hundred years to rear and protect fifty pairs of wild indigenous red kites. Once a scourge over London and as common as magpies in the British harbour ports, the red kite became reduced to only three surviving cocks and hens, limited to an area north of Cors Caron. Efforts to protect them were often unorthodox. Ned Thomas, Pennar Davies and Meredydd Evans broke into a mid-Wales BBC transmitting yard at about the same time as the red kite population reached around forty pairs. After the usual minimal and nominal damage they telephoned the police and waited for their own arrest. Strange ornithologists. Then, when August storms were over and Gwynfor Evans did not have to fast, the new Welsh language broadcasting channel opened with a translation of, of all things, Shane starring Alan Ladd. Later, despite vitriolic ridicule from Labour politicians in the south, four Gogs opened Barcud television studios in Caernarfon. Today Barcud has digital claws and those who attack its work, such as Dr Kim Howells, Labour MP, sound like Matthew Arnold in the 1860s who himself set out poison and traps for those beautiful wild birds he wanted to exterminate.

Wren

A troglodyte but altogether different from the swallow and the swift. Among the roots' eroded eaves the wren's cave always remains below. Those few Welsh Crusaders brought back legends of the *'dryw'*. One, how it could not fly through bushes but had to go beneath them. And the wren does not fly through hedges to this day but stops at the branches, working its way, hopping lower and lower as it forages busily towards the other side. But wrens could fly through wounds, and the wounded Crusader who dreamed of one was sure to recover. Other legends credit the wren with strategy, such as outwitting the king of the birds by hiding in its eagle wing, flying higher for one second, becoming king itself. So powerful is the wren that on St Stephen's Day and on the first wedding anniversary it was hunted through the house by the wildest pack of boys, serving as their target. One of the most delightful logos has always been that of *Llyfrau'r Dryw*, the publishing firm of Aneirin and Alun Talfan Davies in the 1940s. Here the energetic wren is an emblem of how even the smallest breast, when it breathes the air it loves, can fill the most daunting concert hall. Sometimes there is no avoiding the wren and its allegorical links with the fictions of identity.

Welsh Cob

This is the golden pony that the Maid of Llyn y Fan Fach, mother of the Doctors of Myddfai, refused to tether for her mortal husband. The one that Giraldus Cambrensis objected to watching in a delicate embrace. The one that spoke to Arthur saying Culhwch's on his way. The horse that killed and ate a lion while Gwallter ap Maldwyn (knight, 1202-1259) slept behind a stone wall in Armenia. The one that said to Mabon, 'The worst is yet to come.' This is the pony whose boiled fat was gouged out from underneath its jawbone; the smoothed bottoms of sparkling water bottles ground into lamps for those deep eye-sockets gathering dust under the quilted bed where, for most of the year, the folk club's status symbol, its M Fari Lwyd, is hidden in a 'cultural desert'. This is the cob, 500 flat tin miniatures of which were found in Taliesin's grave. This is the cob that decorates the seal of Lowri merch Urien, contemporary installation artist, teaching sculpture in Tel Aviv. This is the cob, no matter how much he whipped his, hers maintained a divine indifference until Pwyll cried out, and began studying active imagination with a horse.

PETER BENNETT

Pigeons

The deeper the shafts the bigger the Belgian pigeon loft. In winter the broken light of a paraffin lamp in the shadow of their quiet wings. Between shifts, in a shed at the top of the allotment, somewhere to sit, smoke and imagine the rest of a life, confined to the butty system, somehow flying free. A man's status and his satisfaction in the length and curl of his pet boar's tusks, the speed of his homing pigeons. That flock, the one coming down below the bald ridgeline, in front of a line of oaks and across the bracken fern, now a blur between the highest terraced rows – one tentative arc around and with a coo and bell-beat of their gliding wings, they close in on the patched-together, fit-for-a-family-of-four, sponsor of local charities, brightly coloured pigeon coop. Bred well, they make a rich and filling pie and, roasted, eaten from a brown paper bag, an endless snack – dark meat thumbed from the bone while walking up the mountain on a Sunday. A photo of the fastest pigeon in the club, *Cosmonaut*, hangs over a tiled fireplace in Maerdy. And a small pillow stuffed with the lightest pigeon feathers – kept as a last resort, like a splinter of the True Cross – ready for when the doctor says it won't be worth calling him out again.

Drover

On his last drive, at the age of forty-eight, whipping a combination of shod oxen and unshod sheep over The Rhigos, Sylvan Pughe, *'porthmon o Gastell Nedd'*, also took with him two maids contracted for work at Abergavenny. Sylvan Pughe was one of the more notable broker/drovers of the Golden Age of Drovers at the end of the first century following the Act of Union, keeping a thorough ledger of his legal and other activities. He had two wives, one at Cirencester and one at Neath. When he died, Pughe's English wife found over a hundred Welsh surety watches in his personal box. His Welsh wife found as many English-made gold watches among Pughe's effects in Wales. The women never met. For all his prudence Pughe died of 'brandy and cigars' among the thimble-riggers of Smithfield Market. His body was returned to Neath. It was not until his English wife faced a bill for 'two score pair of leather shoes' for geese from a saddler in Stroud that she tried more earnestly to trace him. Informed of his death via the tollbooth militia, the English Mrs Pughe remarried, this time to a *porthmon* from Brecon. Bigamy was not unusual among Welsh drovers. It's likely that their wives also enjoyed a vigilant form of polyandry.

Mary Jones

It's a beautiful story and for her, Thomas Charles of Bala – who, every time he wrestled with personal vice came out on top – broke a promise to a friend. Her struggle is well-known – a weaver's daughter, self-taught, newly literate, pulling pennies from the sleeves of the mountains, concealed where no one else thought to look for them. Determined. The famous barefoot miles and, at the end of it, utter disappointment. Charles of Bala founding the British and Foreign Bible Society in the wake of her homespun skirt, its muddy hem turning independently, like the holiest of hermit dervishes, away from her, out like a top through the Empire's thirsty colonies. Charles of Bala, patient, meticulous, starched, clean – his scrupulous diary recording every thought that verged on sin – he loved her and couldn't cut her off. He sold Mary the Good Book. He fully accounted for his transgression to his friend. He made up for it. Monolingual, she came to his parlour wet with the sweat of twenty-six barefoot miles. With a bag of small coins that six years carding wool on Cadair Idris farms had scrimped for her. The struggle victorious, she read, daily, from her trophy for the rest of her life. Charles of Bala took his pen and ink, considered the personal cost, and decided to provide a Bible for every Mary Jones in every country in the world.

D.J., Saunders & Valentine

Nationalists. Patriots. Terrorists. Looters. Soldiers. Ghosts. Merrymakers. Hectorers. Peddlers. Silverfish. Kings. Balladeers. Skivers. Speeders. Dredgers. Puppies-from-underneath-the-floorboards. Futurists. Post-colonialists. Multi-culturalists. Killed. Incarcerated. Blood smeared over the sleeping body of the calumniated feminine. *Gwlad. Gwinllan. Yr Hen Dŷ Ffarm.* Monica. Leaveners. Wasters. Alchemists. Culprits. Boxers. Fakers. Brewers. Conjurers. Fishmongers. Separatists. Victims. Internationalists. Why not lovers? Wisps of camphor. Nose flautists. Devotees. Honeymooners. Flimflam artists. Mountebanks. Triplets. Dissemblers. Redactors. Boffins. Shitheads. Idealists. Malingerers. Tacticians. Banjo players. Tinkers. Land-grabbers. Elitists. Middle-sizers. Strings of silk wet with the sweat of dancing. Fools. Prospectors. Apologists. Poets. Vibrational doctors. Bearers. Charlatans. Memorists. Bonesetters. Bunglers. Martyrs. Paper folders. Undertakers. Who were they? Tuvanian infiltrators? Stabbers. Teachers. Monsters. Compromisers. Dabblers. Collaborators. Shiners. Diviners. Tax dodgers. Crackers. Ranters. Dreamers. They had their names. They had their numbers.

Celtic Cross

The Celtic Cross, as unfamiliar to some as the New York City pretzel is in Wales – not quite the novelty it was. Coils of the Celtic Cross trace themselves back to corded spirals of Bronze Age potters – probably women. Perhaps pretzels too, turning via intestinal flora, make similar connections. Perhaps it's just that time needn't intersect eternity as finally as we thought; that these uneven gears are there to remind us of other Christian possibilities. Cogs in slow relief, favouring cyclical time, not quite abandoning the alternatives of wholesale repetition but, at a different speed, rephrasing Paul's single origin, single wound, single trauma and single explanation. Wheel and shaft, making bread from stone, milling the British earth with its weighted axle turning a northern shadow in the sky. The shafts at Llanilltud Fawr have been dated to the 7th Century and, just as 7th Century bells were not designed to chime, these crosses were not designed to look as though they had no choice. David, Samson and Illtud sat close to them, rubbed their backs on them and followed each alternative, twisted knot while studying them. These won't be mimicked – moulding the Roman Cross into a luminous wheel while their Mabinogi turned from Modron's world to His.

Chapel

No longer the lodging of his cape only, St Martin's cloak hangs alongside mechanic's overalls, arts workshop posters, carpet discount flashcards and unturned calendars. Converted to a second home, its occasional echo insured against secular damage. As close to the land as a molehill, built by builders before architects saw their special opportunity. These emptying granaries where the untrained, spontaneous preachers' words were once so carefully heard. But the diet has changed. No longer tea-parties for a thousand or ten thousand witnesses at Ebenezer's baptismal dunk. No longer crowds of familiar, committed people willing to be together and endure it. Established pressure hated them at the time and mocked each Congregational debt. Their chief rival, as they cave in – millennial deafness and conformity. Preaching dissent and independent bread; it's a diet that, as much as ever, appeals to fools. A soldier giving his cloak to a beggar; colliers inviting ministers down the shaft to pray; the sewing machinist committing an imprudent covenant for an abstraction. An outhouse of God – plain, burned into a steep, unwanted field. Each hand-made, broad-wall, vaulting window calculating this world's costs. The deacons' fort, and behind them each hard bench turned to face the message.

GWEDDI'R ARGLWYDD
EIN TAD YR HWN WYT YN Y NEFOEDD.
SANCTEIDDIER DY ENW.
DELED DY DEYRNAS.
GWNELER DY EWYLLYS MEGIS YN Y NEF,
FELLY AR Y DDAEAR HEFYD.
DYRO INNI HEDDIW EIN BARA BEUNYDDIOL.
A MADDAU I NI EIN DYLEDION, FEL Y
MADDEUWN NINNAU I'N DYLEDWYR.
AC NAC ARWAIN NI I BROFEDIGAETH.
EITHR GWARED NI RHAG DRWG:
CANYS EIDDOT TI YW'R DEYRNAS
A'R NERTH, A'R GOGONIANT,
YN OES OESOEDD. AMEN.

Yr Iaith (Gweddi'r Arglwydd)

It's a serviceable vehicle, a prayer wheel that was never meant to turn, set by the smokeless fireplace, polished once a week with brasso and an old cotton vest. *Cais ddedwydd yn ei gartref* – this particular trophy carried home from a visit to every Llanfair ym Mochnant where Gwydion paused. Its influence felt in every fair in Wales, every seaside rock and sweet shop, every editing suite, every sales room, every lounge and smoke-room. The merit of a brass plaque and on it, *Gweddi'r Arglwydd*. This version, the brass version brought down to tacks by Peter Williams and his popularisation of the Bible. A thin, affordable yellow token, a ticket stub from the journey William Morgan made. It makes a few assumptions – putting its hands together, as He showed them; assuming too that these few words both find a home and homeland and not the exile of an antique shop, skip or the housing department's home clearance van. The doxological *Canys eiddot* added later. Now that the brass is hard to find and not always visible by the mantleshelf there is a heavy irony to *oes oesoedd*. Hung to be seen and read when already it was known by heart. Now that, at weddings and at funerals, the congregation has to look it up, the thin, pressed plate is a mode of transport only the most devoted believe is coming back.

Bearded Male

The bearded male or, in some cases, the severely bearded male, was a common feature of nonconformist life in Victorian Wales. In the early days of photography no family portrait was complete without the enormous beard of a patriach reaching down over his dark lapels. Among the more famous severely bearded Victorian males were Eben Fardd, poet; Daniel Owen, novelist; Michael D. Jones, founder of the Patagonia experiment and Dr William Price, chartist druid and founder of modern cremation. Hair was a valuable commodity in the American settlements and while female emigrants were encouraged to train their hair to grow thick and long, male emigrants cultivated full and impressive beards. This hair could always be made into button baskets when the need arose. Daniel Owen was encouraged to emigrate several times solely on the evidence and appreciation of his particularly fine and silky beard. In one letter to his sponsors at the Wrexham Gazette, Daniel Owen complains of chronic ambiguity towards his beard – an anxiety making him so nervous that he could not write. The clean-shaven Victorian male was a novelty in Wales. During the Great War men in the trenches were made to shave as a precaution against lice. Hedd Wyn, the 'shepherd poet', prided himself on shaving at least twice a week.

Scenic Route

When coastal windows faced into the confined yard, away from the grey and dismal sea, scenery lay inward, via the Bible as guidebook. The first explorer holidays took the Cousin of the Gypsies as their conductor, and copper cutters followed. Best viewed from a Great Little Train, so that the frame remains the same but the framework keeps on moving – confirming that it's just a holiday, justifying the rack of helpful, illustrated leaflets, for the tourist by the tourist. Scenery. Wallpaper. Weekend visits and a well-turned early Polaroid of Celtic crags and Celtic waterfalls. Editing Carneddog and his wife out of the desert landscape. Visitors' disapproval of 'Welsh' Sundays, milkbars and most of all small town trading estates so that (among rock-climbers' targets) local people might actually get a little work. There aren't as many scenic prints hanging in all the pubs of Porth as there are in one quaint Maentwrog 'Inn'. Chopping the landscape into a chop-suey of intricate engravings. Netsuke, prayer-mats, ivory toothpicks, Tibetan slippers and (from a Crafte Shoppe in Betws-y-coed) a photocopied print of 'The Ladies of Llangollen' enlarged out from *Gallant Little Wales* and sold as an original.

ICH
DIEN

Ich Dien

In 1346, following the Battle of Crécy, a 16-year-old man wearing black armour was brought the heraldic gear of one of the defeated dukes of King John of Bohemia. Admiring the single ostrich feather and German motto, and knowing that its former owner had been killed, the boy took the emblem as his own. His claim that the ostrich feather belonged to John himself was not strictly true. But the emblem did originate at the Heraldic Court of King Wenceslas in Prague – which, at that time, received alchemical doctors from Tabriz and Jerusalem. *Ich Dien*, I Serve. The Black Prince's devotion to the Holy Trinity led him to expand the single feather emblem into three ostrich feathers, keeping the original motto and declaring it an official symbol of the Court of the Prince of Wales. In 1370 the Prince sacked, without a formal battle, the surrendered town of Limoges (he was 40 years old). Troubled by flu, fatigue and toothache, the Black Prince – wearing Bohemian ostrich feathers on his horse and shield – ordered the slaughter of every man, woman, child and domestic animal and the looting of the town. In 1969 Charles of Windsor, Prince of Wales, received his Investiture at Caernarfon in Gwynedd. Two council workers, George Taylor and William Alwyn Jones, were killed when their home-made bomb, exploded prematurely near the railway line at Abergele where 21-year-old Charles of Windsor's train was due to pass.

Guardsman's Hat

As Kant said, 'The possession of power inevitably corrupts the free judgement of reason.' Erotism and death. Hence the Welsh Guards' powerful bearskin hat. The armed warrior, hussar or grenadier, cannot rationally consider the pathological enormity of what he is being trained to do and needs a self-effacing cloud. Camouflaged in combat, undistinguished from their comrades, modern Guards still keep the fantastic berserker costume. Given a wicker frame, as light as an hallucination swooning around the head, the enlisted former stores assistant has disappeared. Fighting, even idling between fighting, needs every ritual flourish. Grooming the busby bestows a fine permission to be enormously daring, enormously crude. Kitchener's afterthought in order to get another accent registered at Loos. Just enough to take the mind away from mundane things – this great, astrological wig. It puts things in perspective. Freeing mortal judgement into the immaculate glory of being among those – selfless others – who also dress to die.

The Welch

Berserk for empire, the Welch fusilier, engineer, gunner, borderer, also stuck his bayonet in the crimson globe. Organised a billet, dry and well supplied, just off the main square of the British Army. Mispronounced and thus accommodated – the way Churchill called them Narzis, and so Cymru mutated from being Gwales, Wales and Welsh to the British military variant Welch. Not quite a mercenary – torn on international days between patriotic anthems. First off, because first among those who were steady and reliable – unlikely to lose their heads when props gave way and the roof caved in. Among the first to face the colonised in Aden, Cyprus, Palestine, Nigeria, Singapore, the South Atlantic. Among the last to march in defence of Morfa Bychan. What would Sir Stanley Baker make of it today? Saving Canada in 1812 from United States expansionism. Swollen battalions of the Boer War, when the swelling never went down and Belgian trenches were a perfect opportunity to test the brass bands' repertoire. Cardiff reared no Sir Roger Casement. Neither Mabon nor Niclas y Glais toured the war camps whistling *Unwaith Eto* in prisoners' ears. Military patriotism – Welch soldiers, serving under the Union Jack with a sneaking suspicion they can't see a dragon there. Eraserheads.

Castle

The best known castles in Wales are fortifications of territorial conquest built to silence and subdue Welsh people. Grim, impressive structures – dark, alien, loveless – just like the Welsh Office with its modern version of a civic moat. 1983 was designated as the Year of the Castle in Wales. Also in 1983, against the recommendations of its own advisers, the Welsh Office decided that Wales should have its own version of the big, new quango, English Heritage. Cadw – Welsh Historic Monuments thus emerged directly from the Year of the Castle fiasco which spent four million pounds celebrating the anniversary of a military project devoted to the slaughter of Welsh aristocratic sovereignty. Those who wrote the first Cadw publications such as *The Edwardian Conquest of Wales* were operating in the vanguard of English Heritage. Naturally, as custodians of 'Welsh' heritage, no one at the Cadw library, archive or projects desk actually speaks Welsh. The first trustee of Cadw was the 7th Marquess of Anglesey,, which might explain why all the money went on Beaumaris Castle and why the site of Siwan's grave at Llanfaes was redeveloped as a sewage treatment plant. It's a familiar story. It was a long time ago. Let's put it behind us.

Whitewashed Cottage

The whitewashed cottage by the stream. These days the second home of a family from Manchester; the rural working family having moved to a Barratt Estate built, with sheep grids, at the edge of a market town. The Santiana sailor, about to round Cape Horn, praised the walls of his father's whitewashed cottage and small roses that grew in the wind-cropped garden. Touring poets from the USA have idealised them in Pulitzer prize-winning collections. This is what one Oxford poet, a regular contributor to Poetry Wales, has to say about her second home in Cwm Nantcol, in the heart of Welsh speaking Wales: 'My husband and I naturally feel ourselves to be foreigners. And let me add that neither of us has been made to feel personally uncomfortable because of this. Our Welsh neighbours couldn't be more friendly.' The whitewashed cottage with a few bits of inherited furniture, its television tuned to the noisy Barcud quiz, four tickets for the Doreen Lewis concert and the sound of feet going over the path to work, to clean, to school. Or – the whitewashed cottage, isolated like Joan of Arc, tied to the flavour of petrol and the favour of showing writer friends where to find it on the map. It asks for a black match – black and crispy, the pale cube of unburned wood, between your thumb and fingernail, not guilty of criminal damage.

Welsh Not

It worked well as Welsh Note and Welsh Stick but so much better when the victims hit upon a verb-noun and made it into a rod with which to beat themselves. After all, getting rid of verbs and nouns was why this little engine that could was devised and, very quickly, via primary schools, why it was so widely recommended. The Welsh Lump, as it was first recorded by English schools inspectors, was the invention of a teacher in Flint who, being miserably inadequate, found that he could not teach English to his monolingual pupils. The Lump did it for him and he caned the pupil who wore The Lump and the one who passed it on. So that The Lump licensed the cane and 'their Welsh was quickly thrashed out of them'. One individual, a schoolboy from Llanuwchllyn, did emerge to challenge this lethal, and official, pedagogic linguicide. At the age of twelve, O.M. Edwards never passed the wooden ticket on, and like drinking vinegar, took the daily cane himself. But the Welsh Not, Welsh Lump, Welsh Stick, Welsh Note hung like a Soweto Necklace around too many necks. You can still get thrashed today, murdered in a Cardiff take-away, sacked from work, thrown out of hotels, denied official papers and prosecuted in the courts of Wales. Hard to believe? Telephone CEFN and ask for a list. Never heard of CEFN?

UMA
O
HUD
ANGHARAD
TOMOS
Y Lolfa

Yma o Hyd

It's a genuine slogan – Goedelic to the core. Slou·gan; sluaghghairm, sloghorne; sluagh = host + gairm = cry. Coined for the chorus of a song, of *nosweithiau llawen*, of a drunken festival at Ffostrasol. Since then the title of an account by a young unemployed Welsh-language female imprisoned in Holloway in 1982. A lyric in popular poetry. The resort of politicians – who gave their portion to earning it, and their share towards denying it. No avoiding it. Sung by Ron Davies at the Yes for Wales celebration in the Park Hotel, Cardiff, the night of the Devolution Referendum. Led by Dafydd Iwan. No ambiguity there. But you might be saying High-Ma-Oh-Hud, wondering why it's in this catalogue in the first place. Just like, after living in Wales for eighteen years, the owner of the 'Welsh Photographic Library' asked me, 'What's a Simm-Ann-Ffa-Gahn-Whw?' [*Cymanfa Ganu*]. Just like the Director of the National Museum of Wales, Cardiff Wales Airport, Chief Executive of the Welsh Development Agency, the Land Authority for Wales, Chief Constables of the South and North Wales Police Authorities and just like the Chancellor and Deans of the University of Wales – their collective, famous, outrageous inability to pronounce the names of their homes and the full titles of their jobs. Thanks to those students that chant it, this flimsy slogan, like the raft of the Medusa, sticks in the craw of the University's deceit.

CYM

Craft Shop

This is the graveyard. Tranquilisers fixed and frozen, decided into swollen cubes – convenient but cold and angular to swallow. Where Blarney laps Efnisien's shore. Here political stockings all fall down and the fancy costumes of conditional suffrage and appropriated heritage are finally the naked penny's own. Whispers that have run out of wax. No one forced the shop to become a counterfeit note in its own town. Whom do these useless algorithms serve – making a fool of any sort of choice? Inventory of antiquated lard in an age of pressed rehabilitation. Whose over-polished glass beads were they? Whose milk-dipped sops? Vague shapes passing through the dislocatable jaw, into the till's reptile gullet. Where, disguised as trade, they are better recognised for what they always meant to be. Takings. Anything, at the end of a retail visit on a tour of classified tokens. Merchants showed Sinbad how they took a lump of meat – sometimes the body of a slave – and hurled it at the end of ropes down into the canyon, hauling up precious stones embedded into it. These shops are lumps of meat.

Gorse

It was a joke among established Welsh pioneers in Oregon to set a plate of chopped gorse in front of new arrivals. Like the tumbleweed, travelling via Russian horse feed, gorse found its way west (via Lake Crystal, Minnesota) in the wagons of apple growers anxious to follow the Llewellyn Brothers. As well as apples, Welsh imported gorse flourished along the Oregon coast. At Beaver Creek, the Welsh church has a relationship with gorse similar to that of chapels in Wales. Its roots are almost impossible to remove and at Siloam, Cefn Cribwr, it's told how the chapel plot had to be soaked with oil and torched for two days until the gorse was rooted out. Deacons still tell visiting preachers how the *'tân yn yr eithin'* burns into the pulpit. Huw Evans writes how, in 1870 and 1871, gorse fires near Cwm Eithin burned for three months. These fires eventually penetrated into the peat where they smouldered for over a year. At Cefneithin gorse surrounds the rugby pitch. At Cwmfelineithin, when they became engaged, the young men of that village used to wear sprigs of gorse in their felt hats. And it was from Hugh Meredith who, with others from Pencader, Delaware, established the Welsh Tract in North Carolina, that Benjamin Franklin learned the saying, 'When gorse is out of bloom, kissing's out of season.'

Bracken Fern

When the moors are as red as a bandit's hair, the bracken baler drops its heavy cubes. Each cube as solid and red as a rusted, compressed car – after the magnet and the crusher squeeze them into shape. Dry red, sediment orange, dark brown between the fronds and stalks. Burning bracken in the light of an orange sun. And the soil, golden dry, loamy where the black bracken beaks – its roots – peck and peck, despite spray, harrowing and ploughing under. It can be eradicated. Tractor, harrow and helicopter applied like radium. Harvesting bracken compensates the farmer with stomach cancer which, eating the blanched crozier tips in spring could alleviate – it's said. But the croziers are gone. Their soft green crooks a rare herb while lamb is common. Wil Boots, Llanberis, risked and lost his life recovering rarer ferns, practically bunjee jumping from the crags. Monmouth bracken, divided from the landscape into small corrosive dice, stained with petrol, hauled across the bridges because the bracken hectares there were extinguished long ago.

Welsh Black Cattle

Once Welsh upland cattle were so stringy and skinny one observer wrote that they 'barely deserve to be described as goats'. Those fat in the forest tempted the obsidian knife, turning ghostly white towards their sacrifice – red inside their ears. But Hywel Dda measured his personal wealth in cattle that were wholly black. Far from aurochs – stock became *da* the way that deer, at a dollar, became a 'buck'. The exact weight accountable in meat, milk and hide, thriving, like yak, on a diet of ice and rushes. A cattle raid worth the human life. Iberian Melisius – King Miles – brought them up from Bos Longifrons to Ulster where, out of reach of Rome, they descended until considered too low for mercenary Latin taste. Kenneled in Aberffraw – loyal to rot and rain until Victorian herd books opened like parks before them, comparing full-bodied blacks to an extended 'gentleman's umbrella'. Wide dewlaps, large sunkwell eyes and a rapturously mellow beef. Short fast legs supporting an enormous chest, stopping at nothing – the perfect inside half. Introduced to the United States at a desert farm in Reno, Nevada in 1963. Featured on a 1984 British Royal Mail postage stamp. Integrated primitive, enlisted emigré, *bodlon* among Tasmanian gum trees.

Laverbread

Pliny again – naming northern foods, called it laver. *Bara lawr* washed, washed and washed, then boiled and boiled. Black fruit of the sea. A dollop that Welsh celebrities are famous for preferring to caviar. Their pose, best served with cold toasted bread and a bottle of white Italian wine. Dry against the sea's mineral salt. And, since it travels reasonably well, available everywhere. Tom and Shirley have eaten it in Las Vegas, Dick and Liz in Israel. Anthony Hopkins on set in New York. Bryn Terfel? Well, laverbread is a Glamorgan thing and it's not a Gwynedd food. *Lobscows.* What is *lobscows* the *hwntws* have to ask, only suspecting that it might be a bowl of stew. Lobscows and laverbread. These days laverbread served from south Wales fishvans comes from Scotland. In the east – China, Korea, Japan – shredded, gelatinous laver is spread in the sun and dried on bamboo racks at the seaside, hardening into film-green brittle papers. When moist with soy sauce these *nori* wafers wrap softly, deliciously, like clothing, around small pellets of fish and rice. If you grew up on laverbread, within sight or sound of Swansea Bay – in the Mir Space Station or the Sanitary Fishmarket of Morehead City – if you saw it on the menu, I guarantee you'd order it.

Rarebit

Here they come over the third bridge (the second estuary crossing) wearing colourful red kerchiefs, billowing polka dot blouses, enormous clogs, carrying harps and zithers and look! some are cutting pegs as they walk and sing. In the background, the sound of machine guns, but these migrant families manage to whistle and fal-de-ra as they wander looking for work. Hardship adds an attractive Celtic melancholy to their manners. In the middle of the day they sit at the edge of the motorway, marvelling at the great lorries and their wonderful cargoes. They have no envy of those pokey Bovis Homes just visible above the high roadside dykes and appear to incur no bruises when they are cruelly beaten by other migrant groups. First among all the pickers of modern Europe, these are truly postmodern stateless workers, free to sleep under the northern stars. 'Rabbits' as they are affectionately known. How they love their cheese! Which some, they say, still eat from plates of Roman glass. Most of all they love to cut great slabs of it (with their gleaming Albacete daggers) setting the cheese on chunks of barley bread, roasting this clumsy variation on the pizza over an open fire. Careful, Taff! That ketchup looks a lot like blood! The story goes that one indulgent rogue rolled his gambo (or cart) on wheels made of the best Caerphilly Cheese. The word first enters polite language in 1725 when John Byrom, hymnist and author of the Universal English Shorthand, records eating 'two Welch rarebits – a most unusual supper'.

Bara Brith

Imagine this: picking strawberries in a field near Valencia. The red, heavy, heart-shaped drops wait for your patient hands under their decoy of thick, furry leaves. As your small blue plastic box fills up, a flock of pink flamingoes passes overhead. She is as surprised as you are. When she comes to stand next to you, she puts a strawberry in your mouth. When you are half way through eating it, she reaches up and kisses you. Later, at your favourite place in Wales, you go out with a flask of coffee in the evening. About an hour before the time of day when bats start to stir their wings, the nearby stream carries shadowed light quickly away under the sandy roots of deep, eroded banks. You have made two small loaves of *bara brith* – the colour of oak leaves still thickly clustered on the early autumn trees. Thrushes start to sing. It is so quiet you can hear blackbirds grubbing about between the withering brambles and feathery October grass. You cut the bread, pour coffee and pass them back and fore. You know the bats and snipe by their differently determined erratic bursts of flight. The speckled bread is moist and sticky. When she is half way through eating it, you lean across and kiss her.

Welsh Cakes

Welsh cakes are first mentioned in modern Welsh literature in the sixteenth century as part of a list of military victuals. Before that, the best hint we have of them is from an Irish document that gives a fuller version of one of the stories from the Mabinogion. There the Welsh cake or picws ar y maen is clearly associated with iron. In the Second Branch Welsh sources refer to an Iron House in which the monstrous couple *Kymideu Kymeinvoll* and her husband *Llassar Llaesgyvnewid* were imprisoned and baked. The Irish source tells how, as the floor of the Iron House became hot, *Kymideu Kymeinvoll* took eggs, flour and salt, mixed them and teased her torturers by producing delicious smelling cakes. Her husband remonstrated with her, complaining that the smell, as well as tormenting their gaolers, made him homesick. But the *picws ar y maen*, he said, were improved for being burned on iron, as opposed to being more slowly turned on stone. This apparently simple dialogue suggests that Welsh cakes predate the Goedelic-Brythonic division and also predate the use of iron itself. The famous drover William Protheroe used Welsh cakes, a fishing line and salmon net for catching bats at Dan yr Ogof caves. Protheroe made a syrup from the bats which he rubbed over his body as part of his conjuring show.

The Severn Bridge

It was at the first bridge, built in Chepstow by Adam Darby in 1785, that I saw a man of the following description – he would let one of his lips drop upon his belly, while he turned the other like a cap upon his head. We had just come from a café and I was standing near the river with my father and my Uncle John, and I heard my father say to John (unbelievably), 'Perhaps there are a lot of men like that in these parts.' I knew then that I was well on the way to Ernst Cassirer country. We were on a trip to London with the Cefn Cribwr Division of the St John's Ambulance Brigade. (There were still mines and quarries and that year Cefn Cribwr won the Grand Priory British Championship.) The Awst suspension bridge was being built and everyone on the coach stood up to get a glimpse as we drove along the A48. The M-fortification of south Wales in the name of late 20th century consumerism was just getting underway. *A fo ben bid bont.* By the time of the third Severn crossing there was also Hinkley Point Nuclear Power Station and less naive enthusiasm. A justifiable streak of suspicion that thousands of acres of estuary wetlands were about to be annihilated forever somehow tempered the value of scurrying back and fore. That the bridges were 'good for Wales' could no longer be simply accepted.

Excalibur

(for Richard Gwyn)

We learn, thanks to Ibn Fadlan from Baghdad, of the importance battle magic played in the lives of Celtic merchants. Ibn Fadlan records the ritual preparations of trading Celts in the 10th century as he observed them at various ports along the Rhine. Weapons and skulls were a central feature of altars built to propitiate Celtic gods. Victory in battle, being the warrior's ultimate obligation, could be achieved only by investing arms with accumulated magic. Goronwy Pebr's spear succeeds in killing Lleu Llaw Gyffes because of the fate or *ghiese* that Lleu betrays into it. Excalibur was the most magic sword of all. Offered by a female hand reaching up from the lake, and accepted as readily as though it had been drawn from stone, it bestowed a ferocious invincibility upon the King. *Caledfwlch*, with nothing dainty or chivalrous about it, the coy magic of its origin carefully disguising its gruesome work. Its reputation came from severed heads and from carefully wounding the surrendered shoulders of fully armed supplicants. When its blade broke, Arthur also broke and Bedwyr, chained to the blade's purple gore, couldn't throw it back. Bedwyr's difficult release of the broken haft countering Arthur's easy hold on both the magic swords he owned. Without enchantment through his weapons, no soldier could hope to find fame via either life or death, hence the enfeebling and fatal distress of Arthur's knight, Teithi Hen ap Gwynnan, because the handle of his knife kept breaking off.

Arthur

Of all the claims that are made on him, this much is certain. Arthur was Culhwch's barber, and we first meet him in Welsh. In the White Book of Rhydderch, Arthur takes his shears out and, fair play, both envies and admires Culhwch's desire for Olwen enough to go with him and challenge Ysbyddaden so that Culhwch can win her for his bride. This may have been when Goonbell was *Gwaunbell*, when Ursa Major was no further than your elbow, when animals could talk and when wishes could come true. Arthur's friends are unfailingly crazy – their nicknames a frenzy of already eccentric jabbering – a sure sign that Arthur is King and can afford to surround himself with dwarves, wizards, nano-specialists, sleeve pullers, thieves, bankers, berserkers, well-sinkers, ship designers, cavaliers, sword swallowers, pint cadgers and the desperately sick. Culhwch bursts in on Arthur and is calmly welcomed like one more iron filing to the North Pole's freakish court. Who wouldn't go there, aged sixteen, just to check out if this is the best place to get a haircut! It still is. Magic, dreams, spirit and the body whirl around Arthur's head; that undifferentiated mind unaffected by all that it allows to navigate.

Guinevere

She had a twin; Pwyll wasn't the only old Welsh monarch to visit the Celtic otherworld. Arthur, easily duped, could never tell, nor even considered that she might not be she, nor where her other was while he, carousing with her scheming substitute – disguised by apple cheeks, bow lips and plaits – toasted perry wine to Camelot. Who was she? Her dowry a round table, when most other tables were still a space between the straw straight onto the smoothed and beaten earth. All this defeated even them, and all inadequate descriptions of her come down to us today via riddles, twins, double dates and the dissimulations of oaths and frailty. When her hair turned white, her age, combined with beauty and sagacity, became so appalling and appealing that princes mistook her for a maid, and kings risked hoping she still might influence their destiny. Having sipped from the Grail, Gwalchmai fab Gwyar moved between her shifting forms – ageless – able to repeat those things he heard about her – her promises, bargains, silences and tactful withdrawal to the convent, laying jewellery aside towards her funeral. So many versions exist because there were as many versions while she lived.

YMDEITHAS
R IAITH
ETH A CH
CYMDEITHAS CYFAM
Gwyl Werin y Cnapan
Dyffryn Teifi

Commemorative Mug

They sat around drinking tea and coffee from patriotic mugs. Odd, but as they chatted, smoked and drank – setting each mug down on an old receipt, a beermat, the carpet, the top of the piano, an empty chair, on a tricky space at the edge of the overcrowded table – the D-shaped handles broke off in their hands. One by one, one at a time. Unreal. Spooky. At first funny, but then difficult to laugh. The end of an era – their struggle told via the slogans of commemorative mugs no longer needed. From now on we'll all be swimming in champagne! The unknown artist honoured, and that mug, which might have been a monument to kitsch, tossed in the bin. The great festival, self-financing and that mug put in the glasshouse – a pity to throw it away. Political prisoners freed, their documents issued in that problematic language (problematic for whom?) – those mugs trashed by the palette load, to the sound of city bells rung for an hour at midnight and at noon. Each mug that might have chained them slipping free of its own accord – goodbye, thank you, you don't need us any more.

Daffodil

The daffodil may indeed be an appropriate flower for a nation that has not flexed its muscles for over four hundred years. Except in the realm of cultural activities Wales has not acted as a unified political unit since the days of Owain Glyndŵr. Until Gwyn Alf's difficult and famous question, *When Was Wales?* many of its citizens deluded themselves that Wales had, during these lean years, all along bleated with one voice. A true condition of pseudo-narcissism. Now that a kind of European peace and the decline of Empire allows some regional freedoms, Wales may perhaps encourage its national flower to split, moderate, develop and multiply from the bulb into a responsible, loving, occasionally reckless form of self-respect. The kind of self-esteem that desires its share of grace and a share in global rewards, having suffered so many accusations of inadequacy. Experience of interminable sensual thrift and of curbs on natural vanity become, via the daffodil, an opportunity to spread some Cambrian light. That the daffodil is a genuine golden yellow is a tribute to its lack of relationship with suffering. The daffodil doesn't care about complaints.

Acknowledgements

Thanks to curators, archivists and photographers at the following agencies, public and private collections for permission to use the following photographs. Often a photograph may not be filed under these titles but according to general category. This list refers to each photograph acccording to its location in this book with further indications in brackets as to how the original may be located in its home collection.

Harp, Tiger Bay, Coracle, Miner's Lamp (Bwllfa Colliers), Pit Head Wheel (Welsh Pit Disaster) [and cover], Crown, Eisteddfod Chair, Teapot, Welsh Dresser, Drover, Chapel, Ich Dien (Cambrian Railway), Welsh Not, Small Beer: National Museums and Galleries of Wales.
Welsh Hat, Rugby, Sheep, Corgi, Greyhound, Bard, Mary Jones, D.J. Saunders & Valentine, Bearded Male (Mr Roberts, Telynor), Castle (Dinefwr), Whitewashed Cottage, Miner's Lamp (cover): The National Library of Wales.
Slate, Red Kite, Wren, Cob, Bearskin (Welsh Guards): *The Western Mail.*
Hill, The Valleys, Lovespoon, Celtic Cross: Pat Aithee.
Ffotograff, Cardiff.
Welsh Rarebit, *Bara Brith*, Welsh Cakes, Commemorative Mug: Carole Mason.
Dragon, Scenic Route, Eisteddfod Chairing Ceremony (cover), Castle (cover): Wales Tourist Board.
Gorse, Bracken Fern, Daffodil: Ian-Sant.
Excalibur, Arthur, Guinevere: BBC Wales, Llandaf.
Welsh Lady (Salem): Walker Art Gallery, Liverpool.
Cardiff Arms Park: Mark Jones.
Buried City of Kenfig: Royal Commission of Ancient and Historical Monuments in Wales.
Sheepdog: Tim Collier.
Cymanfa Ganu, grateful thanks to all who helped try and locate a source for this photograph, taken from the Delyse LP, A Nation Sings 1963.

How Green Was My Valley, British Film Institute.
River Taff: Jeff Edwards, The National Environment Agency.
Male Choir (Pendyrys): John H. Lewis, Secretary, Pendyrys Male Voice Choir.
Rain: Telegraph Colour Library.
Eisteddfod Plate: William McClure Brown.
Dawns Llangrannog: Iola Jones, Adran Adnoddau, Urdd Gobaith Cymru.
Pigeon: G. D. Butler, photo by Peter Bennet.
The Welch: thanks to Bryn Owen, Welch Regiment Museum, Cardiff.
Yma o Hyd: Y Lolfa.
Welsh Black Cattle: Jenny Buckton, photo Jim Treasure, Australia.
Laverbread: Welsh Foods Agency.
Severn Bridge: J.M. Clune, Severn River Crossing Plc.
Leek, Coal, Stone Circle, Dwynwen, Tea Towel, *Yr Iaith*, Craft Shop: David Greenslade